Dear Parents and Guardians,

As we gather around the warmth of the Christmas season, we are reminded of the timeless stories that have shaped our faith and values. This advent calendar is more than just a collection of tales; it is a journey through the rich tapestry of the Old Testament, designed to bring the wisdom and wonder of these ancient stories to your children.

Each day, as you share these stories with your little ones, you are not only teaching them about the past but also instilling in them the virtues of faith, hope, and love. These stories are a gift that will grow with them, guiding them through life's many adventures.

May this book be a cherished part of your family's holiday traditions, bringing joy and inspiration to your home. Thank you for allowing me to be a part of your Christmas celebration.

A Special Request

If you and your children enjoy this advent calendar, I would be grateful if you could take a moment to leave me a review on Amazon.

Your feedback helps me to continue creating meaningful and engaging content for families like yours.

MERRY CHRISTMAS

"Train up a child in the way he should go; even when he is old he will not depart from it."

- Proverbs 22:6

Day 1

God Creates the World

In the beginning, there was nothing. No light, no sky, no earth, no sea, no animals, no people. Just darkness. But then, God came!

God said, "Let there be light!" And suddenly, there was a brilliant flash, and the darkness disappeared. God saw that the light was good, and He separated it from the darkness. He called the light "day" and the darkness "night."

Then, God created the sky, separating the waters above from the waters below. He made the land and filled it with plants – tall trees, colorful flowers, and soft grasses. He created the sun, moon, and stars to light up the sky and mark the days and nights.

Next, God filled the waters with amazing creatures – fish that swam in the seas, birds that soared through the air. He made all sorts of animals to walk and crawl on the land – big and small, furry and scaly.

Finally, God said, "Let us make mankind in our image." So God created the first humans, a man and a woman. He gave them the special job of taking care of the earth and all its creatures.
God looked at everything He had made, and it was very good! He was happy with His creation, and He rested on the seventh day.

Think about it:

- What is your favorite thing that God created?
- How can you help take care of God's creation?

Day 2
Adam and Eve in the Garden

After God created the world, He made a special garden called Eden. It was a beautiful place with sparkling rivers, delicious fruits, and amazing animals. In the middle of the garden, God planted two special trees: the Tree of Life and the Tree of the Knowledge of Good and Evil.

God placed the first man, Adam, in the garden to take care of it. But Adam was lonely, so God created Eve from Adam's rib. Now Adam had a friend! They could explore the garden together, name the animals, and enjoy all the wonderful things God had made.

God told Adam and Eve they could eat fruit from any tree in the garden except one – the Tree of the Knowledge of Good and Evil. "If you eat from that tree," God warned, "you will surely die."
One day, a sneaky snake slithered up to Eve. "Did God really say you can't eat from any tree in the garden?" the snake asked.

Eve replied, "We can eat from any tree except the Tree of the Knowledge of Good and Evil. God said if we eat from it, we will die."

The snake hissed, "That's not true! You won't die. God knows that if you eat the fruit, you will become wise like Him."

Eve looked at the fruit. It looked so delicious! She couldn't resist. She took a bite and gave some to Adam, and he ate it too.

Suddenly, Adam and Eve felt ashamed. They realized they were naked, and they tried to hide from God. Because they disobeyed God, they were no longer allowed to stay in the beautiful garden.

Think about it:
- Why do you think Adam and Eve disobeyed God?
- What are some things that tempt you to do wrong?

Day 3
Cain and Abel

Adam and Eve had two sons, Cain and Abel. Cain grew up to be a farmer, and Abel became a shepherd. One day, they both decided to bring gifts to God. Cain brought some of the fruits and vegetables he had grown, while Abel brought the best lamb from his flock.

God was pleased with Abel's gift because Abel gave his very best to God. But God wasn't pleased with Cain's gift. Maybe Cain didn't give his best, or maybe his heart wasn't in the right place.

This made Cain very angry. He was so jealous of his brother that his face grew dark and his heart filled with rage. God saw this and said to Cain, "Why are you angry? If you do what is right, you will be accepted. But if you don't do what is right, sin is crouching at your door. It wants to control you, but you must master it."

But Cain didn't listen. He tricked Abel into going out to the fields with him, and there, in a fit of anger, Cain killed his brother.

When God asked Cain where Abel was, Cain lied and said, "I don't know. Am I my brother's keeper?"

But God knew what Cain had done. "What have you done?" God said. "Listen! Your brother's blood cries out to me from the ground. Now you are under a curse and driven from the ground, which opened its mouth to receive your brother's blood from your hand."

Cain was very afraid and ran away. God put a mark on Cain to protect him, but Cain had to live with the consequences of his sin.

Think about it:
- Why was Cain angry with Abel?
- How can we control our anger when we feel jealous or upset?

Day 4

Noah's Ark and the Flood

As time passed, people began to do more and more bad things. God saw that the world was filled with wickedness, and it made Him very sad.

But there was one good man named Noah. Noah loved God and always tried to do what was right. God said to Noah, "I am going to send a great flood to cover the whole earth. But I will save you and your family."

God told Noah to build a huge boat called an ark. He gave Noah exact instructions on how to build it – big enough to hold Noah's family and two of every kind of animal. Noah obeyed God and built the ark just as God had commanded.

Then, God told Noah to bring his wife, his three sons, and their wives into the ark. He also told Noah to bring seven pairs of every kind of clean animal and one pair of every kind of unclean animal, along with enough food for everyone.

When everyone was safely inside the ark, the rain started to fall. It rained for forty days and forty nights! The water rose higher and higher until the whole earth was covered. All the wicked people and the animals outside the ark were swept away.

But Noah, his family, and the animals in the ark were safe. They floated on the water for many months until the rain stopped and the water began to go down. Finally, the ark came to rest on top of a mountain

Noah sent out a dove to see if the land was dry. The dove returned with an olive branch in its beak, a sign that the water was receding. When the earth was dry, God told Noah to leave the ark with his family and all the animals.

God was pleased with Noah. He promised never to flood the earth again and placed a beautiful rainbow in the sky as a sign of His promise.

Think about it:
- Why did God send the flood?
- What does the rainbow remind us of?

Day 5

The Tower of Babel

After the flood, Noah's family grew and grew, and people spread all over the earth. They all spoke the same language and decided to build a city with a huge tower that reached all the way to heaven. They wanted to make a name for themselves and be famous.

They said, "Let's build a city with a tower that reaches to the sky. This will keep us together and make us famous!"

They began to build their tower, using bricks and tar to make it strong and tall. Higher and higher it rose, but God saw what they were doing.

God knew that if people were united with one language and purpose, they could become powerful and do whatever they wanted, even bad things. He wanted people to spread out and fill the earth, not stay together in one place.

So, God came down and confused their language. Suddenly, people couldn't understand each other anymore! They spoke different languages, and it was impossible to continue building the tower. The people were confused and frustrated. They couldn't work together anymore, so they abandoned their city and the tower and scattered all over the earth.

That's how the different languages of the world came to be. The city was called Babel, which means "confusion."

Think about it:

- Why did the people want to build the tower?
- Why did God confuse their language?

Day 6

God's Promise to Abraham

Abraham was a man who loved God. One day, God spoke to Abraham and said, "Leave your country, your people, and your father's household and go to the land I will show you. I will make you into a great nation, and I will bless you; I will make your name great, and you will be a blessing. I will bless those who bless you, and whoever curses you I will curse; and all peoples on earth will be blessed through you."

Abraham trusted God, so he packed up his belongings and his family and set off on a long journey to a new land that God would show him. This land was called Canaan.

God appeared to Abraham again and said, "To your offspring I will give this land." But Abraham was old, and his wife, Sarah, was also very old. They had no children.

Abraham asked God, "How can I be sure that I will have descendants and inherit this land?"

God took Abraham outside and said, "Look up at the sky and count the stars—if indeed you can count them." Then he said to him, "So shall your offspring be."

Abraham believed God's promise. He knew that God would keep His word, even though it seemed impossible.

And God did keep His promise! Abraham and Sarah had a son named Isaac, and through Isaac, Abraham had many descendants. They became a great nation, just as God had promised.

Think about it:

- Why did Abraham obey God and leave his home?
- What did God promise Abraham?

Day 7

Abraham's Big Test

God wanted to test Abraham's faith and trust. He called out to Abraham and said, "Abraham!"

"Here I am," Abraham replied.

Then God said, "Take your son, your only son, Isaac, whom you love, and go to the region of Moriah. Sacrifice him there as a burnt offering on a mountain I will show you."

This was a very difficult thing for Abraham to do. He loved Isaac very much. But Abraham trusted God and knew that God would provide. So he obeyed.

Early the next morning, Abraham got up and prepared for the journey. He took Isaac and two of his servants and set off for the mountain that God had shown him.

After three days, they arrived at the foot of the mountain. Abraham told his servants to stay behind and said to Isaac, "We will go and worship, and then we will come back to you."

Abraham and Isaac climbed the mountain together. Isaac carried the wood for the fire, and Abraham carried the fire and a knife. As they walked, Isaac asked, "Father, the fire and wood are here, but where is the lamb for the burnt offering?"

Abraham replied, "God himself will provide the lamb for the burnt offering, my son."

When they reached the top of the mountain, Abraham built an altar and arranged the wood on it. Then he bound Isaac and laid him on the altar. Abraham took the knife and was about to sacrifice his son when suddenly, an angel of the Lord called out from heaven, "Abraham! Abraham!"

"Here I am," Abraham replied.

"Do not lay a hand on the boy," the angel said. "Do not do anything to him. Now I know that you fear God, because you have not withheld from me your son, your only son."

Abraham looked up and saw a ram caught in a thicket. He took the ram and sacrificed it as a burnt offering instead of his son.

Abraham was so happy and thankful that God had provided. He named that place "The Lord Will Provide."

Think about it:
- Why did God ask Abraham to sacrifice Isaac?
- How did Abraham show his trust in God?

Day 8

Jacob and Esau

Isaac, the son of Abraham, grew up and had twin sons named Esau and Jacob. Esau was the older brother, and he was a skillful hunter, a man of the open country. Jacob was a quiet man, staying among the tents.

One day, Esau came in from the open country, famished. He saw Jacob cooking some delicious stew and said, "Quick, let me have some of that red stew! I'm starving!"

Jacob replied, "First sell me your birthright."

The birthright was a special privilege given to the firstborn son. It meant that he would inherit a larger share of his father's possessions and become the leader of the family.

Esau was so hungry that he didn't care about his birthright. He said, "Look, I am about to die! What good is a birthright to me?"

So Jacob said, "Swear to me first." So Esau swore an oath to him, selling his birthright to Jacob. Then Jacob gave Esau some bread and some lentil stew. He ate and drank, and then got up and left.

Years later, when Isaac was old and his eyesight was failing, he called Esau and said, "My son, go out to the fields and hunt some wild game for me. Prepare me

the kind of tasty food I like and bring it to me to eat, so that I may give you my blessing before I die."

Rebekah, their mother, overheard this conversation. She wanted Jacob to receive the blessing instead of Esau. So she quickly prepared some tasty food and told Jacob to take it to his father, pretending to be Esau.

Jacob was hesitant, but he obeyed his mother. He put on Esau's clothes and covered his hands and neck with goatskins to feel hairy like Esau. Then he took the food to his father.

Isaac was suspicious. "Who are you, my son?" he asked.

Jacob lied and said, "I am Esau your firstborn."

Isaac felt Jacob's hands and said, "The voice is the voice of Jacob, but the hands are the hands of Esau." He was still unsure, but he ate the food and gave Jacob his blessing.

When Esau returned and discovered what had happened, he was furious. He cried out with a loud and bitter cry and said to his father, "Bless me—me too, my father!"

Isaac was distressed and said, "Your brother came deceitfully and took your blessing."

Esau held a grudge against Jacob for stealing his blessing.

Think about it:
- Why did Jacob want Esau's birthright?
- Was it right for Jacob to trick his father?

Day 9

Joseph's Dreams and his Brothers' Jealousy

Jacob had twelve sons, but his favorite was Joseph. He even gave Joseph a beautiful, multi-colored coat as a special gift. This made Joseph's brothers very jealous.

One night, Joseph had a strange dream. He dreamed that he and his brothers were tying sheaves of grain in the field. Suddenly, Joseph's sheaf stood up straight, and all his brothers' sheaves bowed down to it.

When Joseph told his brothers about his dream, they were furious. "What do you mean, your sheaf stood up and our sheaves bowed down to yours? Do you think you will rule over us?" they sneered. Another time, Joseph had another dream. This time, he dreamed that the sun, moon, and eleven stars bowed down to him. He told his father and his brothers about this dream, and they were even angrier.

Jacob scolded Joseph, "What is this dream you had? Will your mother and I and your brothers actually come and bow down to the ground before you?"

But Jacob kept thinking about Joseph's dreams, wondering what they meant.

One day, Joseph's brothers were taking care of their father's sheep far away from home. Jacob said to Joseph, "Go and see if your brothers and the flocks are well, and bring me word."

Joseph set off to find his brothers. When they saw him coming, they were filled with jealousy and hatred. "Here comes that dreamer!" they said. "Let's kill him and throw him into a pit. We can say that a wild animal ate him. Then we'll see what becomes of his dreams!"

Reuben, the oldest brother, tried to save Joseph. "Let's not take his life," he said. "Don't shed any blood. Throw him into this cistern here in the wilderness, but don't lay a hand on him." Reuben planned to come back later and rescue Joseph.

When Joseph arrived, his brothers grabbed him, tore off his beautiful coat, and threw him into the empty cistern.

Later, some merchants passed by on their way to Egypt. Judah, another brother, suggested, "What will we gain if we kill our brother and cover up his blood? Come, let's sell him to the Ishmaelites and not lay our hands on him; after all, he is our brother, our own flesh and blood." His brothers agreed.

So they pulled Joseph up out of the cistern and sold him to the merchants for twenty shekels of silver. The merchants took Joseph to Egypt.

Think about it:
- Why were Joseph's brothers jealous of him?
- What did they do to Joseph?

Day 10

Joseph in Egypt

The merchants took Joseph to Egypt and sold him as a slave to a powerful man named Potiphar, an officer of Pharaoh, the king of Egypt.

Even though Joseph was a slave, God was with him. Joseph was a hard worker, and Potiphar saw that he was honest and trustworthy. Soon, Potiphar put Joseph in charge of his entire household.

But Potiphar's wife tried to trick Joseph into doing wrong. When Joseph refused, she falsely accused him, and Joseph was thrown into prison.

But even in prison, God was with Joseph. The prison warden saw that Joseph was a good and wise man, so he put Joseph in charge of all the other prisoners.

One day, two of Pharaoh's officers, the cupbearer and the baker, were also thrown into prison. Both of them had strange dreams, and they were troubled because they didn't understand what the dreams meant.

Joseph said to them, "Don't worry, God can help us understand your dreams. Tell me your dreams."

The cupbearer told his dream first. He dreamed that he saw a vine with three branches. The branches blossomed, and grapes appeared.

He took the grapes and squeezed them into Pharaoh's cup and gave the cup to Pharaoh.

Joseph said, "This is what your dream means: The three branches are three days. Within three days, Pharaoh will lift up your head and restore you to your position. You will put Pharaoh's cup in his hand, just as you used to do when you were his cupbearer. But please remember me when it goes well with you. Mention me to Pharaoh and get me out of this prison."

Then the baker told his dream. He dreamed he was carrying three baskets of bread on his head. Birds were eating the bread out of the baskets.

Joseph said, "This is what your dream means: The three baskets are three days. Within three days, Pharaoh will lift off your head and impale your body on a pole. And the birds will eat away your flesh."

Three days later, it happened just as Joseph had said. Pharaoh restored the cupbearer to his position, but he impaled the baker. Unfortunately, the cupbearer forgot all about Joseph.

Two years later, Pharaoh had two very disturbing dreams. In the first dream, he saw seven healthy cows come up out of the Nile River, followed by seven thin and ugly cows. The thin cows ate the healthy cows!

In the second dream, Pharaoh saw seven heads of healthy grain growing on a single stalk. Then seven heads of thin and scorched grain sprouted after them. The thin heads of grain swallowed up the seven healthy and full heads.

Pharaoh was very troubled by these dreams, and none of his wise men or magicians could explain them. Then the cupbearer finally remembered Joseph! He told Pharaoh about Joseph's ability to interpret dreams.

Pharaoh immediately sent for Joseph. Joseph explained that the dreams meant that Egypt would have seven years of plenty followed by seven years of famine.

He advised Pharaoh to store up grain during the years of plenty to prepare for the famine.

Pharaoh was so impressed with Joseph's wisdom that he put Joseph in charge of all the land of Egypt!

Think about it:
- How did God help Joseph even when he was a slave and a prisoner?
- What important job did Pharaoh give Joseph?

Day 11

Joseph Forgives His Brothers

The famine that Joseph had predicted came to the land of Canaan where his father and brothers lived. Food became scarce, and Jacob's family was running out of grain.

Jacob heard that there was grain in Egypt, so he sent his sons, except for his youngest son Benjamin, to buy some.

When Joseph's brothers arrived in Egypt, they didn't recognize him. They bowed down before him, just as Joseph had dreamed many years ago.

Joseph remembered his dreams and knew that these were his brothers. He spoke harshly to them, accusing them of being spies.

The brothers were terrified and tried to explain that they were honest men, just trying to buy food for their family. They told Joseph about their father and their younger brother, Benjamin.

Joseph saw the remorse in their hearts and wanted to know if they had truly changed. He devised a plan to test them. He kept Simeon as a hostage and told them to bring Benjamin to Egypt.

The brothers returned home with heavy hearts and told their father everything that had happened. Jacob was heartbroken that Simeon was being held captive and refused to let Benjamin go.

But the famine grew worse, and they were running out of food. Finally, Jacob reluctantly agreed to let Benjamin go with his brothers back to Egypt.

When Joseph saw Benjamin, his own brother from the same mother, he was overcome with emotion. He ordered a feast to be prepared for his brothers.

The next day, Joseph secretly placed his silver cup in Benjamin's sack. Then he sent his brothers on their way. But he soon sent his steward after them, accusing them of stealing the cup.

The brothers were shocked and afraid. They searched their sacks, and the cup was found in Benjamin's sack. They returned to Joseph, pleading for mercy.

Judah stepped forward and offered to take Benjamin's place, showing that he had changed and was willing to sacrifice himself for his brother.

Joseph could no longer contain himself. He sent all his servants out of the room and cried out, "I am Joseph! Is my father still living?"

His brothers were stunned and speechless. Joseph said to them, "Come close to me." When they had done so, he said, "I am your brother Joseph, the one you sold into Egypt! And now, do not be distressed and do not be angry with yourselves for selling me here, because it was to save lives that God sent me ahead of you."

Then Joseph threw his arms around his brothers and wept. He forgave them for what they had done and reassured them that it was all part of God's plan.

Think about it:
- Why did Joseph test his brothers?
- How did Joseph show forgiveness to his brothers?

Day 12

Baby Moses is Rescued

Many years passed, and Joseph and his brothers died. The Israelites, Joseph's people, continued to live in Egypt. They had many children and became a large and powerful nation.

A new Pharaoh began to rule Egypt. He didn't remember Joseph or all the good things Joseph had done for Egypt. This Pharaoh was afraid of the Israelites because they were so numerous. He thought they might become more powerful than the Egyptians.

So Pharaoh made the Israelites slaves. He forced them to work very hard, building cities and doing other difficult tasks. But the more the Egyptians oppressed them, the more the Israelites multiplied and spread.

Pharaoh became even more afraid. He ordered that all baby boys born to the Israelites be thrown into the Nile River. He wanted to prevent the Israelites from growing any stronger.

During this time, a baby boy was born to an Israelite family. His mother saw that he was a beautiful baby, and she hid him for three months. But when she could no longer hide him, she made a plan to save his life.

She took a basket made of reeds and waterproofed it with tar and pitch. She placed the baby in the basket and set it among the reeds along the bank of

the Nile River. Then, the baby's older sister, Miriam, stood at a distance to see what would happen.

Pharaoh's daughter came down to the Nile to bathe. She saw the basket among the reeds and sent her servant girl to get it. When she opened the basket, she saw the baby crying, and she felt sorry for him. "This is one of the Hebrew babies," she said.

Then Miriam approached the princess and asked, "Shall I go and get one of the Hebrew women to nurse the baby for you?"

"Yes, go," the princess said.

Miriam ran and got her own mother, the baby's mother! The princess said to the woman, "Take this baby and nurse him for me, and I will pay you."

So the woman took the baby and nursed him. When the child grew older, she brought him to Pharaoh's daughter, and he became her son. She named him Moses, which means "drawn out of the water."

Think about it:
- Why did Pharaoh order that the Israelite baby boys be killed?
- How was Moses saved?

Day 13

The Burning Bush

Moses had grown up in Pharaoh's palace, but he knew he was an Israelite. One day, he saw an Egyptian beating an Israelite slave. Moses became angry and defended the Israelite, but he ended up killing the Egyptian.

Pharaoh found out and was very angry with Moses, so Moses had to run away from Egypt. He went far away to a land called Midian.

In Midian, Moses got married and became a shepherd, taking care of sheep. One day, he was leading his flock to the far side of the desert, near a mountain called Horeb.

Suddenly, Moses saw an amazing sight! There was a bush on fire, but it wasn't burning up! The flames were bright, but the bush was not being destroyed.

Moses was curious. He said to himself, "What is this? I must go over and see this strange sight. Why isn't the bush burning up?"

Can you write me the seconf half of this story so it seems seemless (Moses had grown up in Pharaoh's palace, but he knew he was an Israelite. One day, he saw an Egyptian beating an Israelite slave.Moses became angry and defended the Israelite, but he ended up killing the Egyptian.

Pharaoh found out and was very angry with Moses, so Moses had to run away from Egypt. He went far away to a land called Midian.

In Midian, Moses got married and became a shepherd, taking care of sheep. One day, he was leading his flock to the far side of the desert, near a mountain called Horeb.

Suddenly, Moses saw an amazing sight! There was a bush on fire, but it wasn't burning up! The flames were bright, but the bush was not being destroyed.

Moses was curious. He said to himself, "What is this? I must go over and see this strange sight. Why isn't the bush burning up?"

As Moses got closer to the burning bush...) Where you talk about: God reveals his name: God tells Moses that his name is "I AM WHO I AM." This signifies that God is eternal and unchanging.

God gives Moses a mission: God tells Moses to go back to Egypt and lead the Israelites out of slavery. Moses is afraid and makes excuses, but God reassures him and promises to be with him.

God gives Moses signs: God gives Moses three signs to perform to prove his authority: turning his staff into a snake, making his hand leprous, and turning water into blood.

Moses obeys: Despite his fears, Moses obeys God and returns to Egypt to confront Pharaoh and begin the process of freeing the Israelites.

Think about it:
- How do you think Moses felt when God asked him to go back to Egypt?
- Have you ever felt scared to do something that you knew was right?

Day 14

The Ten Plagues

Moses returned to Egypt with his brother, Aaron, and they went to see Pharaoh. They told Pharaoh that God had said, "Let my people go, so that they may worship me in the desert."

But Pharaoh was stubborn and refused to let the Israelites go. He said, "Who is the Lord, that I should obey him and let Israel go? I do not know the Lord and I will not let Israel go."

So God sent ten plagues on Egypt to show Pharaoh His power and convince him to free the Israelites.

1. Water turned to blood: All the water in Egypt, even in the jars and bowls, turned to blood! The fish died, and the river smelled terrible.
2. Frogs: Hordes of frogs hopped everywhere – into the houses, bedrooms, and even the ovens and kneading troughs!
3. Gnats: Swarms of tiny biting gnats filled the air and covered the people and animals, causing great discomfort.
4. Flies: Thick swarms of flies buzzed everywhere, making life miserable for the Egyptians.
5. Disease on livestock: The Egyptians' livestock – horses, donkeys, camels, cattle, sheep, and goats – became sick and died.
6. Boils: Painful boils broke out on the Egyptians and their animals.
7. Hail: A terrible hailstorm with thunder and lightning destroyed crops and buildings.
8. Locusts: Huge swarms of locusts ate everything that was left of the crops and plants.

1. Locusts: Huge swarms of locusts ate everything that was left of the crops and plants.
2. Darkness: A thick darkness covered the land of Egypt for three days. People couldn't see each other, and no one could move around.
3. Death of the firstborn: The final plague was the most devastating. The angel of death passed over Egypt, and the firstborn son in every Egyptian family died, even Pharaoh's own son.

After each plague, Pharaoh would beg Moses and Aaron to ask God to stop it. He would promise to let the Israelites go, but as soon as the plague stopped, he would change his mind and refuse again.

Finally, after the tenth plague, Pharaoh was heartbroken and terrified. He called for Moses and Aaron in the middle of the night and said, "Up! Leave my people, you and the Israelites! Go, worship the Lord as you have requested. Take your flocks and herds, as you have said, and go. And also bless me."

At last, Pharaoh let the Israelites go free!

Think about it:

- Why did God send the plagues on Egypt?
- How did the plagues show God's power?
- What can we learn about God from this story?

Day 15

The Passover

Even though Pharaoh had finally agreed to let the Israelites go, God knew that he might change his mind again. So God planned one final plague, the worst one yet. But this time, He would protect the Israelites.

God told Moses to instruct the Israelites to prepare for a special meal called the Passover. Each family was to choose a perfect lamb without any blemishes. They were to slaughter the lamb and put some of its blood on the sides and tops of their doorframes.

Then, they were to roast the lamb and eat it with unleavened bread (bread made without yeast) and bitter herbs. They were to eat this meal quickly, with their sandals on their feet and their staffs in their hands, ready to leave Egypt.

God said, "When I see the blood on the doorframes, I will pass over that house. The plague of death will not touch you when I strike the land of Egypt."

The Israelites did exactly as God commanded. They prepared the Passover meal and ate it together. That night, the angel of death passed through the land of Egypt. In every Egyptian household, the firstborn son died, from the firstborn of Pharaoh to the firstborn of the prisoner in jail, and even the firstborn of all the livestock.

But when the angel of death saw the blood on the doorframes of the Israelite houses, he passed over them. No one inside those houses was harmed.

There was a great cry of grief throughout Egypt, but the Israelites were safe. Pharaoh and all the Egyptians were terrified. They urged the Israelites to leave quickly, taking all their possessions with them.

The Israelites left Egypt in a hurry, just as God had commanded. They were finally free!

Think about it:
- Why did God instruct the Israelites to celebrate the Passover?
- What does the blood on the doorframes represent?
- How does this story show God's protection and love for His people?

Day 16

Crossing the Red Sea

The Israelites left Egypt with all their belongings, but Pharaoh quickly regretted letting them go. He gathered his army and chased after them with chariots and horsemen.

The Israelites were terrified when they saw the Egyptian army approaching. They cried out to Moses, "Was it because there were no graves in Egypt that you brought us to the desert to die? What have you done to us by bringing us out of Egypt?"

Moses reassured them, "Do not be afraid. Stand firm and you will see the deliverance the Lord will bring you today. The Egyptians you see today you will never see again. The Lord will fight for you; you need only to be still."

Then God told Moses, "Raise your staff and stretch out your hand over the sea to divide the water so that the Israelites can go through the sea on dry ground."

Moses obeyed, and a strong east wind blew all night, pushing the water back and creating a dry path through the sea. The Israelites walked through the sea on dry ground, with walls of water on their right and on their left!

The Egyptians pursued them, following them into the sea with their chariots and horsemen. But God threw the Egyptian army into confusion. Their chariot wheels

became clogged, and they cried out, "Let's get away from the Israelites! The Lord is fighting for them against Egypt."

Then God told Moses, "Stretch out your hand over the sea so that the waters may flow back over the Egyptians and their chariots and horsemen."

Moses stretched out his hand over the sea, and at daybreak the water returned to its place. The Egyptians tried to flee, but the Lord swept them into the sea. The water flowed back and covered the chariots and horsemen—the entire army of Pharaoh that had followed the Israelites into the sea. Not one of them survived!

But the Israelites had crossed the sea safely on dry ground. They had witnessed the awesome power of God and His deliverance from slavery.

Think about it:
- How did the Israelites feel when they saw the Egyptian army?
- How did God protect the Israelites?
- What does this story teach us about God's power and love?

Day 17

The Ten Commandments

After crossing the Red Sea, the Israelites journeyed through the desert towards the Promised Land. They traveled for three months and finally came to Mount Sinai.

God called Moses to the top of the mountain. There, amidst thunder and lightning, God spoke to Moses and gave him ten important rules to live by. These rules are called the Ten Commandments.

God said:

1. "You shall have no other gods before me." This means that we should worship only God and not put anything or anyone else in His place.

2. "You shall not make for yourself an image in the form of anything in heaven above or on the earth beneath or in the waters below. You shall not bow down to them or worship them." We should not make idols or statues to worship.

3. "You shall not misuse the name of the Lord your God." We should always treat God's name with respect.

4. "Remember the Sabbath day by keeping it holy. Six days you shall labor and do all your work, but the seventh day is a sabbath to the Lord your God." We should set aside one day a week to rest and worship God.

5. "Honor your father and your mother." We should respect and obey our parents.

6. "You shall not murder." We should not take another person's life.

7. "You shall not commit adultery." We should be faithful in our relationships.

8. "You shall not steal." We should not take things that don't belong to us.

9. "You shall not give false testimony against your neighbor." We should always tell the truth.

10. "You shall not covet your neighbor's house. You shall not covet your neighbor's wife, or his male or female servant, his ox or donkey, or anything that belongs to your neighbor." We should be content with what we have and not be jealous of others.

God gave these commandments to the Israelites to help them live good lives and be His special people.

Think about it:

- Why do you think God gave the Ten Commandments?
- Which commandment do you think is the most important?
- How can you follow the Ten Commandments in your everyday life?

Day 18

The Golden Calf

While Moses was on Mount Sinai receiving the commandments from God, the Israelites grew impatient. They gathered around Aaron and said, "Come, make us gods who will go before us. As for this fellow Moses who brought us up out of Egypt, we don't know what has happened to him."

Aaron answered them, "Take off the gold earrings that your wives, your sons, and your daughters are wearing, and bring them to me." So all the people took off their earrings and brought them to Aaron. He took what they handed him and made it into an idol cast in the shape of a calf, fashioning it with a tool. Then they said, "These are your gods, Israel, who brought you up out of Egypt."

When Aaron saw this, he built an altar in front of the calf and announced, "Tomorrow there will be a festival to the Lord." So the next day the people rose early and sacrificed burnt offerings and presented fellowship offerings. Afterward, they sat down to eat and drink and got up to indulge in revelry.

Meanwhile, on the mountain, God told Moses, "Go down, because your people, whom you brought up out of Egypt, have become corrupt. They have been quick to turn away from what I commanded them and have made themselves an idol cast in the shape of a calf. They have bowed down to it and sacrificed to it and have said, 'These are your gods, Israel, who brought you up out of Egypt.'"

Moses turned and went down the mountain with the two tablets of the covenant law in his hands. When he approached the camp and saw the calf and the dancing, his anger burned, and he threw the tablets out of his hands, breaking them to pieces at the foot of the mountain. He took the calf the people had made and burned it in the fire; then he ground it to powder, scattered it on the water, and made the Israelites drink it.

The next day, Moses said to the people, "You have committed a great sin. But now I will go up to the Lord; perhaps I can make atonement for your sin." So Moses went back to the Lord and said, "Oh, what a great sin these people have committed! They have made themselves gods of gold. But now, please forgive their sin—but if not, then blot me out of the book you have written."

The Lord replied to Moses, "Whoever has sinned against me I will blot out of my book. Now go, lead the people to the place I spoke of, and my angel will go before you. However, when the time comes for me to punish, I will punish them for their sin." And the Lord struck the people with a plague because of what they did with the calf Aaron had made.

Day 19

The Tabernacle

After receiving the Ten Commandments, God wanted to dwell among His people, the Israelites. He instructed Moses to build a special tent called the Tabernacle. This would be a portable sanctuary where God's presence would reside.

God gave Moses detailed instructions on how to build the Tabernacle. He told him the exact dimensions, the materials to use, and the furnishings to include.

The Israelites were eager to help build the Tabernacle. They generously brought offerings of gold, silver, bronze, blue, purple, and scarlet yarn, fine linen, goats' hair, ram skins dyed red, and acacia wood. They also brought spices, olive oil for the lampstand, spices for the anointing oil and for the fragrant incense, and precious stones to decorate the breastpiece and the ephod.

Skilled craftsmen and women worked together to build the Tabernacle according to God's design. They constructed the tent with its coverings, the Ark of the Covenant to hold the Ten Commandments, the table for the bread of the Presence, the golden lampstand, the altar of incense, the altar of burnt offering, the bronze basin for washing, and all the other furnishings.

When the Tabernacle was completed, the cloud of the Lord's presence descended and covered it. The glory of the Lord filled the Tabernacle, and Moses could not enter the Tent of Meeting because the cloud had settled on it.

From then on, the cloud of the Lord's presence would rest on the Tabernacle during the day, and fire would appear in the cloud at night. Whenever the cloud lifted from above the Tabernacle, the Israelites would set out on their journey. But if the cloud did not lift, they would not set out—until the day it lifted.

The Tabernacle became the center of worship for the Israelites. It was a visible reminder of God's presence among them and His covenant with them.

Think about it:

- Why did God want the Israelites to build the Tabernacle?
- What were some of the special furnishings inside the Tabernacle?
- How did the Tabernacle show God's presence with His people?

Day 20

The Bronze Serpent

The Israelites continued their journey through the desert, but they became impatient and complained against God and Moses. They said, "Why have you brought us up out of Egypt to die in the wilderness? There is no bread! There is no water! And we detest this miserable food!"

God was angry with the Israelites for their complaining and lack of trust. He sent venomous snakes among them, and many people were bitten and died.

The people realized their sin and came to Moses, pleading, "We have sinned by speaking against the Lord and against you. Pray that the Lord will take the snakes away from us." So Moses prayed for the people.

Then the Lord said to Moses, "Make a snake and put it up on a pole; anyone who is bitten can look at it and live."
So Moses made a bronze serpent and put it up on a pole. Then when anyone was bitten by a snake and looked at the bronze serpent, they lived.

Think about it:
- Why did God send the snakes among the Israelites?
- How did the bronze serpent save the people?
- What does this story teach us about sin and forgiveness?

Day 21

Spies in the Promised Land

After wandering in the wilderness for many years, the Israelites were finally approaching the Promised Land, the land of Canaan that God had promised to Abraham.

Moses chose twelve men, one from each tribe of Israel, to go as spies and explore the land. He instructed them to observe the land, the people, the cities, and the strength of their fortifications. He also told them to bring back some of the fruit of the land.

The spies traveled throughout Canaan for forty days, gathering information. They saw that the land was indeed fertile and abundant, flowing with milk and honey. They even cut down a branch with a single cluster of grapes so large that two of them had to carry it on a pole between them! They also brought back some pomegranates and figs.

However, ten of the spies were afraid. They saw that the people living in Canaan were strong and lived in large, fortified cities. They said to Moses, "We can't attack those people; they are stronger than we are... We seemed like grasshoppers in our own eyes, and we looked the same to them."

But two of the spies, Caleb and Joshua, had faith in God. They said, "We should go up and take possession of the land, for we can certainly do it... The Lord is with us. Do not be afraid of them."

The Israelites listened to the ten fearful spies and grumbled against Moses and Aaron.

They even talked about choosing a new leader to take them back to Egypt!

God was angry with the Israelites for their lack of faith. He declared that none of the adults who had left Egypt would enter the Promised Land, except for Caleb and Joshua. They would wander in the wilderness for forty years until that generation had passed away.

Think about it:
- Why did Moses send spies to the Promised Land?
- Why were the ten spies afraid?
- How did Caleb and Joshua show their faith in God?
- What can we learn about the importance of trusting God, even when things seem difficult?

Joshua and the Battle of Jericho

After the Israelites had successfully spied out the Promised Land and received encouraging reports, they were ready to begin their conquest. Joshua, their leader, was given specific instructions by God on how to take the city of Jericho, a heavily fortified city that stood as a significant obstacle in their path.

Now Jericho was tightly shut up because of the Israelites. No one went out and no one came in. Then the Lord said to Joshua, "See, I have delivered Jericho into your hands, along with its king and its fighting men. March around the city once with all the armed men. Do this for six days. Have seven priests carry trumpets of rams' horns in front of the ark. On the seventh day, march around the city seven times, with the priests blowing the trumpets. When you hear them sound a long blast on the trumpets, have all the people give a loud shout; then the wall of the city will collapse and the people will go up, every man straight in."

Joshua called the priests and said to them, "Take up the ark of the covenant of the Lord and have seven priests carry trumpets in front of it." And he ordered the army, "Advance! March around the city, with an armed guard going ahead of the ark of the Lord."

For six days, the Israelites marched around the city once each day, with the priests blowing their trumpets. The armed guard marched ahead of the priests who blew the trumpets, and the rear guard followed the ark. All this time, the trumpets were sounding, but Joshua had commanded the army, "Do not give a war cry, do not raise your voices, do not say a word until the day I tell you to shout. Then shout!"

On the seventh day, they got up at daybreak and marched around the city seven times in the same manner, except that on that day they circled the city seven times. The seventh time around, when the priests sounded the trumpet blast, Joshua commanded the army, "Shout! For the Lord has given you the city! The city and all that is in it are to be devoted to the Lord."

When the trumpets sounded, the people shouted, and at the sound of the trumpet, when the people gave a loud shout, the wall collapsed; so every man charged straight in, and they took the city. They devoted the city to the Lord and destroyed with the sword every living thing in it—men and women, young and old, cattle, sheep, and donkeys

Think about it:
- What was the significance of the priests blowing the trumpets and the people shouting?
- What can we learn about the importance of following God's instructions, even when they seem unusual or difficult?

Day 23

Deborah the Judge

After the Israelites had been disobedient to God, they were ruled by a mean king named Jabin. His army commander, Sisera, had many iron chariots and treated the Israelites very badly for twenty years. The Israelites prayed to God for help.

Deborah was a wise and brave woman who was a judge and a prophet. She helped the Israelites with their problems and gave them God's messages. One day, God told Deborah to call a man named Barak. She told Barak, "God commands you to take ten thousand men and go to Mount Tabor. God will help you defeat Sisera and his army."

Barak said, "I will go, but only if you go with me."

Deborah agreed to go with Barak, but she told him, "Because you asked me to come, the honor of defeating Sisera will go to a woman."

Barak gathered his men and went to Mount Tabor. When Sisera heard about it, he brought his chariots and soldiers to fight. Deborah told Barak, "Go! Today is the day God will help you defeat Sisera." Barak and his men charged down the mountain, and God helped them win the battle. Sisera's army was defeated, and Sisera ran away on foot.

Sisera ran to the tent of a woman named Jael. She invited him in and gave him some milk to drink.

Sisera was very tired and fell asleep. While he was sleeping, Jael took a tent peg and a hammer and quietly went to him. She drove the peg into his head, and Sisera died.

When Barak came looking for Sisera, Jael showed him what she had done. That day, God helped the Israelites defeat King Jabin and his army. Deborah and Barak sang a song of praise to God for the victory.

Think about it:
- Why did the Israelites pray to God for help?
- How did Deborah show her bravery and faith in God?
- Why did Barak want Deborah to go with him?
- What can we learn about trusting and obeying God, even when we are scared?

Day 24

Gideon and the Fleece

The Israelites were in trouble again because they had turned away from God. This time, they were being bullied by the Midianites. God chose a man named Gideon to help save the Israelites. But Gideon was unsure if he was the right person for the job.

One night, Gideon prayed to God and said, "If you really want me to save Israel, please give me a sign. I will put a fleece of wool on the ground. If the fleece is wet with dew in the morning, but the ground is dry, then I will know you will help me save Israel."

The next morning, Gideon got up early and checked the fleece. It was soaking wet, but the ground around it was dry! Gideon squeezed the fleece and wrung out a bowlful of water.

But Gideon still wasn't sure. He prayed again, "Please don't be angry with me, God. Let me ask for one more sign. This time, let the fleece be dry and the ground be covered with dew."

God was patient with Gideon. The next morning, Gideon found the fleece dry and the ground wet with dew. Now Gideon knew that God would help him save Israel.

Encouraged by these signs, Gideon gathered an army to fight the Midianites. But God told Gideon he had too many men. God wanted to show that the victory would come from Him, not from the size of the army. So Gideon sent home anyone who was afraid.

Then God told Gideon to take the men down to the water to drink. Only those who lapped the water with their hands to their mouths were chosen. This left Gideon with just 300 men.

With this small army, Gideon prepared to fight. God gave Gideon a plan. He divided the 300 men into three groups and gave each man a trumpet and an empty jar with a torch inside. During the night, they surrounded the Midianite camp. At Gideon's signal, they blew their trumpets, smashed the jars, and shouted, "A sword for the Lord and for Gideon!"

The Midianites were terrified and confused. They turned on each other with their swords and fled. God had given Gideon and the Israelites a great victory with just 300 men.

Think about it:
- Why did Gideon ask God for signs with the fleece?
- How did God show patience and understanding with Gideon?
- Why did God reduce the size of Gideon's army?
- What can we learn about trusting God and following His plans, even when they seem unusual or difficult?

Thank You

Dear Readers,

Thank you for joining me on this journey through the Old Testament. I hope these stories have brought joy, wisdom, and a deeper understanding of faith to your family.

A Final Request

If you enjoyed this advent calendar, I would be incredibly grateful if you could share your thoughts by leaving a review on Amazon. Your feedback not only helps me improve but also assists other families in discovering and enjoying this book.

Wishing you continued blessings and a joyful journey in faith,

Made in United States
Orlando, FL
22 November 2024

54299556R00048